Practical
Pre-School

Planning
for Learning
through
SPRING

Rachel Sparks Linfield and Penny Coltman

Illustrated by Cathy Hughes

Contents

2-3   Making plans

4-7   Using the Desirable Outcomes for Children's Learning

8-9   Week 1 Detecting Spring

10-11   Week 2 Frogs

12-13   Week 3 Spring rain

14-15   Week 4 Woolly week

16-17   Week 5 Mothers' Day

18-19   Week 6 Spring parade

20   Bringing it all together - Spring parade

21   Resources

22   Collecting evidence

23   Six-week skills chart

24   Home links

Inside back cover   Parent's page

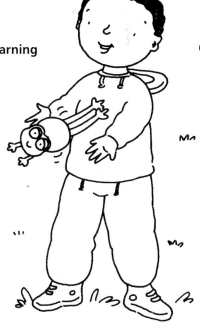

Published by Step Forward Publishing Limited

35b Park Court, Park Street, Leamington Spa, CV32 4QN   Tel: 01926 420046

© Step Forward Publishing Limited 1998

Planning for Learning through Spring   ISBN: 1-902438-04-3

MAKING PLANS

WHY PLAN?

The purpose of planning is to make sure that all children enjoy a broad and balanced curriculum. All planning should be useful. Plans are working documents which you spend time preparing, but which should later repay your efforts. Try to be concise. This will help you in finding information quickly when you need it.

LONG TERM PLANS

Preparing a long-term plan, which maps out the curriculum during a year or even two, will help you to ensure that you are providing a variety of activities and are meeting the statutory requirements of the Desirable Outcomes for Children's Learning on entering compulsory education (1997).

Your long-term plan need not be detailed. Divide the time period over which you are planning into fairly equal sections, such as half terms. Choose a topic for each section. Young children benefit from making links between the new ideas they encounter so as you select each topic, think about the time of year in which you plan to do it. A topic about minibeasts will not be very successful in November!

Although each topic will address all the learning areas, some could focus on a specific area. For example, a topic on Spring lends itself well to activities relating to knowledge and understanding of the living world. Another topic might particularly encourage the appreciation of stories. Try to make sure that you provide a variety of topics in your long-term plans.

Autumn 1	Me and my family
Autumn 2	Toys/Christmas
Spring 1	Once upon a time
Spring 2	Spring
Summer 1	Change
Summer 2	Out and about

MEDIUM TERM PLANS

Medium term plans will outline the contents of a topic in a little more detail. One way to start this process is by brainstorming on a large piece of paper. Work with your team writing down all the activities you can think of which are relevant to the topic. As you do this it may become clear that some activities go well together. Think about dividing them into themes, the topic of Spring for example has themes such as detecting Spring, frogs and Spring rain.

At this stage it is helpful to make a chart. Write the theme ideas down the side of the chart and put a different area of learning at the top of each column. Now you can insert your brainstormed ideas and will quickly see where there are gaps. As you complete the chart take account of children's earlier experiences and provide opportunities for them to progress.

Refer back to the Desirable Outcomes document and check that you have addressed as many different aspects of it as you can. Once all your medium-term plans are complete make sure that there are no neglected areas.

MAKING PLANS

DAY TO DAY PLANS

The plans you make for each day will outline aspects such as:
- resources needed;
- the way in which you might introduce activities;
- the organisation of adult help;
- size of the group;
- timing.

Identify the learning which each activity is intended to promote. Make a note of any assessments or observations which you are likely to carry out. On your plans make notes of which activities were particularly successful, or any changes you would make another time.

A FINAL NOTE

Planning should be seen as flexible. Not all groups meet every day, and not all children attend every day. Any part of the plans in this book can be used independently, stretched over a longer period or condensed to meet the needs of any group. You will almost certainly adapt the activities as children respond to them in different ways and bring their own ideas, interests and enthusiasms. Be prepared to be flexible over timing as some ideas prove more popular than others. The important thing is to ensure that the children are provided with a varied and enjoyable curriculum which meets their individual developing needs.

USING THE BOOK

- Collect or prepare suggested resources as listed on page 21.

- Read the section which outlines links to the Desirable Outcomes document (pages 4 - 7) and explains the rationale for the topic of Spring.

- For each weekly theme two activities are described in detail as examples to help you in your planning and preparation. Key vocabulary, questions and learning opportunities are identified.

- The skills chart on page 23 will help you to see at a glance which aspects of children's development are being addressed as a focus each week.

- As children take part in the Spring topic activities, their learning will progress. Collecting evidence on page 22 explains how you might monitor children's achievements.

- Find out on page 20 how the topic can be brought together in a grand finale involving parents, children and friends.

- There is additional material to support the working partnership of families and children in the form of a home links page, and a photocopiable parent's page found at the back of the book.

It is important to appreciate that the ideas presented in this book will only be a part of your planning. Many activities which will be taking place as routine in your group may not be mentioned. For example, it is assumed that sand, dough, water, puzzles, floor toys and large scale apparatus are part of the ongoing pre-school experience. Role play areas, stories, rhymes and singing, and group discussion times are similarly assumed to be happening in each week although they may not be a focus for described activities.

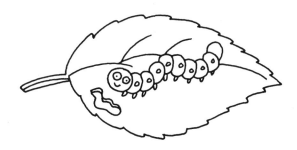

USING THE DESIRABLE OUTCOMES FOR CHILDREN'S LEARNING

Having decided on your topic and made your medium term plans you can use the document produced by the Department of Education and Employment called *Desirable Outcomes for Children's Learning on entering compulsory education* to highlight the key learning opportunities your activities will address. The desirable outcomes are split into six areas: Personal and Social Development, Language and Literacy, Mathematics, Knowledge and Understanding of the World, Physical Development and Creative Development. Do not expect each of your topics to cover every outcome but your long-term plans should allow for all the outcomes to be addressed.

The following section highlights parts of the desirable outcomes document in point form to show what children are expected to be able to do by the time they enter compulsory education in each area of learning. These points will be used throughout this book to show how activities for a topic on Spring link to these expectations. For example, Personal and Social Development point 2 is 'work as part of a group and independently'. Activities suggested which provide the opportunity for children to do this will have the reference PS2. This will enable you to see which parts of the desirable outcomes are covered in a given week and plan for areas to be revisited and developed.

In addition you can ensure that activities offer variety in the outcomes to be encountered. Often a similar activity may be carried out to achieve different learning outcomes. For example, when going on a walk to detect signs of Spring children will be able to develop aspects of Knowledge and Understanding of the World. They can also be encouraged to work as a group, to explore new learning and to treat living things and the environment with care. In this way children will at the same time be furthering their Personal and Social Development. It is important therefore that activities have clearly defined learning outcomes so that these may be emphasised during the activity and for recording purposes.

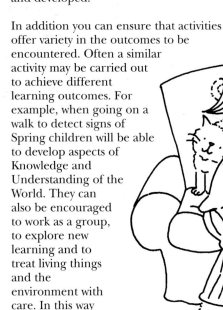

PERSONAL AND SOCIAL DEVELOPMENT (PS)

These outcomes consider important aspects of development which affect the ways children learn, behave and relate to others.

Children will:

PS1 be confident, show appropriate self-respect and establish effective relationships with other children and with adults

PS2 work as part of a group and independently

PS3 concentrate and persevere in their learning and seek help where needed

PS4 be eager to explore new learning and show ability to initiate ideas and solve simple problems

PS5 demonstrate independence in selecting an activity or resources and in dressing and personal hygiene

PS6 be sensitive to the needs and feelings of others and show respect for people of other cultures and beliefs

PS7 take turns and share fairly

PS8 express their feelings and behave in appropriate ways developing an understanding of what is right, what is wrong and why

PS9 treat living things properly and their environment with care and concern

PS10 respond to relevant cultural and religious events and show a range of feelings such as wonder, joy or sorrow, in response to their experiences of the world

The topic of Spring provides valuable opportunities for children to treat living things properly and to show concern for their local environment. Children will be encouraged to be sensitive to the needs and feelings of others by activities which involve thinking of carers around the time of Mothers' Day. Inevitably many outcomes will also develop as a natural result of activities in other key areas. For example, when children collaborate to play games within Mathematics and Physical Development they will also have the opportunity to further PS2.

L8 recognise their own names and some familiar words

L9 recognise letters of the alphabet by shape and sound

L10 use pictures, symbols, familiar words and letters to communicate meaning

L11 develop an awareness of some of the purposes of writing

L12 write their names with appropriate use of upper and lower case letters

The activities suggested for the topic of Spring provide the opportunity for children to respond to a variety of imaginative situations including stories and role play. Through looking at books and listening to stories such as *The Very Hungry Caterpillar* and *Five Minutes' Peace* children will be able to respond to and enjoy books. The making of group big books will enable them to know how books are organised. The writing of greetings for cards and name labels for pictures will help children to develop their early writing skills. Throughout all the activities children will be encouraged to communicate fluently and with meaning.

LANGUAGE AND LITERACY (L)

The Language and Literacy outcomes provide the basis for developing children's ability to read and write with enthusiasm, interest and confidence.

Children will:

L1 use a growing vocabulary with increasing fluency to express thoughts and convey meaning to the listener

L2 listen and respond to stories, songs, nursery rhymes and poems

L3 participate in role play with confidence

L4 enjoy books and handle them carefully

L5 understand how books are organised

L6 know that words and pictures carry meaning

L7 begin to associate sounds and patterns in rhymes, with syllables and with written words and letters

MATHEMATICS (M)

These outcomes cover important aspects of mathematical understanding and provide the foundation for numeracy. They focus on achievement through practical activities and on using and understanding language in the development of simple mathematical ideas.

Children will:

M1 use mathematical language, such as circle, in front of, bigger than and more, to describe shape, position, size and quantity

M2 recognise and recreate patterns

M3 be familiar with number rhymes, songs, stories, counting games and activities

M4 compare, sort, match, order, sequence and count using everyday objects

M5 recognise and use numbers to 10 and are familiar with larger numbers from their everyday lives

M6 begin to use their developing mathematical understanding to solve practical problems

M7 through practical activities understand and record numbers, begin to show awareness of number operations, such as addition and subtraction, and begin to use the language involved

As children carry out the activities in this topic, seasonal artefacts, songs and images are used to introduce and reinforce the fundamental counting skills of number awareness and one-to-one matching. The development of mathematical vocabulary is a priority and the importance of encouraging children to talk about their first-hand experiences is emphasised throughout the topic. Through water play children explore aspects of capacity. Measurement and pattern are similarly encountered in relevant contexts.

KNOWLEDGE AND UNDERSTANDING OF THE WORLD (K)

Children will:

K1 talk about where they live, their environment, their families and past and present events in their own lives

K2 explore and recognise features of living things, objects and events in the natural and made world

K3 look closely at similarities, differences, patterns and change

K4 show awareness of the purposes of some features of the area in which they live

K5 talk about observations, recording them sometimes

K6 ask questions to gain information about why things happen and how things work

K7 explore and select materials and equipment

K8 use skills such as cutting, joining, folding and building for a variety of purposes

K9 use technology where appropriate to support learning

The topic of Spring provides ample opportunity for children to explore and recognise features of living things. Activities which relate to both the natural and the made world will encourage children to look at similarities and differences. Children will further their ability to use skills such as cutting, joining and building through making nests and cress bonnets. Throughout all the activities children should be given the chance to talk about their observations and to ask questions.

PHYSICAL DEVELOPMENT (PD)

These outcomes explore a wide range of fine and gross motor skills which are useful throughout all areas of life.

Children will:

PD1   move confidently and imaginatively with increasing control and co-ordination and an awareness of space and others

PD2   use a range of small and large equipment and balancing and climbing apparatus, with increasing skill

PD3   handle appropriate tools, objects, construction and malleable materials safely and with increasing control

Activities involving mime and dance are used thematically to support children's developing abilities to express their ideas and feelings through movement. Gross motor skills are also encouraged through games and the use of large apparatus. As children manipulate materials in a variety of 'making' activities they will develop fine muscle control and co-ordination.

CREATIVE DEVELOPMENT (C)

Children will:

C1   explore sound and colour, texture, shape, form and space in two and three dimensions

C2   respond in a variety of ways to what they see, hear, smell, touch and feel

C3   through art, music and dance, stories and imaginative play show an increasing ability to use their imagination, to listen and to observe

C4   use a widening range of materials, suitable tools, instruments and other resources to express ideas and to communicate their feelings

During this topic children will experience working with a variety of materials as they make models, prepare some seasonal edible treats and explore a range of art and craft activities. Close observation is encouraged with children recording their ideas using a variety of media. Model ponds, for example, are constructed collaboratively using everyday recycled materials. Weather conditions are used to stimulate imaginative responses with children making their own sounds to imitate spring showers.

Week 1
DETECTING SPRING

PERSONAL AND SOCIAL DEVELOPMENT

- Look at a large picture of a Spring-time scene (trees in blossom, Spring flowers, children playing outside). Discuss what children can do in Spring that they cannot do in Winter. Talk about how children feel in the Spring. What are their favourite activities? (PS8, 10)

- Discuss festivals which children in the group celebrate during Spring. These might include Easter (Christian), Baisakhi (Sikh), Holi (Hindu), Passover (Jewish). Invite parents to come and talk to children about the celebrations. (PS1, 6)

LANGUAGE AND LITERACY

- Read *The Very Hungry Caterpillar* by Eric Carle (Picture Puffin). Make a group version based on children's favourite foods. (L2, 4, 5)

- In preparation for the Physical Development activity based on bulbs read *The Tiny Seed* by Eric Carle (Hamish Hamilton/Puffin). Talk about the changes that took place. Discuss the differences between Spring and Winter and Spring and Summer. (L1, 2)

- Make a spring picnic role play area. Securely fix a tight string at ceiling height across a corner of the room. Cut across an unopened roll of green crepe paper every 1-2 cm. Without unrolling these sections encourage the children to help you to twist them. Then shake them open to make long twisty fronds. Dangle these from the string, packing them fairly closely, and introducing paler greens, pinks and whites. The end result is a weeping blossom tree which encloses an area. Place a picnic rug and tea set on the floor. Children love the feel of moving through the tree curtain to reach this special place. (L3)

MATHEMATICS

- Use the group's version of *The Very Hungry Caterpillar* to practise counting. Ask questions such as 'How many apples did the caterpillar eat?'. (M5, 6)

- With the help of children make a number frieze with a Spring theme: one blossom tree, two lambs, three baby rabbits, four eggs in a nest, five ducklings on a pond etc. On each picture display clearly the corresponding numeral. (M5)

KNOWLEDGE AND UNDERSTANDING OF THE WORLD

- Choose a fine day to go for a Spring walk. Look for signs of Spring such as nests, leaves emerging from the earth, buds on twigs and minibeasts. Once back inside encourage children to describe what they saw and to record their observations in drawings and paintings. (K1, 3, 5)

- Use bulbs planted the previous term to show children how bulbs shoot and grow into plants. Explain that you are going to look at the plants each day. Make a timeline for the bulbs. Begin with a large display showing a plant pot and green shoots cut from sugar paper. Each week add other pots which show how the shoots have grown and the leaves and flowers starting to appear. (K2, 3, 5)

- Make nests - see activity opposite. (K2, 6, 8)

PHYSICAL DEVELOPMENT

- Mime being a bulb changing during Spring. Encourage slow, controlled movement. (PD1)

- Choose a nice day to use outdoor toys that were put away for the winter. Afterwards, encourage children to talk about the experience. (PD2)

- Encourage children to be hungry caterpillars searching for food as they crawl and slither through hoops and larger apparatus with holes. (PD1)

CREATIVE DEVELOPMENT

- Use buds found in pot-pourri to make collages of trees in blossom. Encourage children to look at real trees in blossom (or use pictures) and to describe the colours and scent. (C1)

- Observe real daffodils. Encourage children to look closely at them, to count petals and leaves and explain that they will be making accurate models of the daffodils. Use egg cartons or bun cases for the trumpet, yellow card petals, green card leaves and green straws. Write children's names on the leaves before arranging them in a large vase. (C1)

ACTIVITY: Being bulbs

Learning opportunity: Moving with control and imagination. Listening to instructions.

Desirable Learning Outcome: Physical Development. Children will move confidently and imaginatively with increasing control and co-ordination as they pretend to be bulbs bursting into life.

Resources: *The Tiny Seed* by Eric Carle (Hamish Hamilton/Puffin).

Organisation: Whole group in a large space.

Key vocabulary: Bulb, shoots, bud, flower.

WHAT TO DO:

Talk to children about Spring being a time of new life. Remind them of the signs of Spring they saw on their walk. Show children the pictures in the book for the part of the story relating to Spring and talk about what is happening.

Explain that the children are going to be bulbs, turning into shoots, growing buds and finally bursting into flower. Talk about the kinds of shapes children will need to make themselves into.

Ask children to be a bulb (tightly curled up), a shoot (long and thin), roots growing under ground (wriggle toes), in bud (clenched fist), in flower (open hands, tall and stretched). As children try each stage praise those who make controlled, clear shapes.

Talk to the children about how plants grow over time and that things happen gradually. Repeat the mime but this time tell the story of the bulb, encouraging children to listen to the details and to change gradually and smoothly.

ACTIVITY: Making nests

Learning opportunity: Recognising features of nests, selecting materials and building nests.

Desirable Learning Outcome: Knowledge and Understanding. Children will observe and recognise features of nests. They will select materials to make a nest.

Resources: Pictures of common birds and birds' nests; old nests; a range of materials for making nests including made and natural materials.

Organisation: Small group.

Key vocabulary: Twigs, grass, moss, nest, soft, safe, warm.

WHAT TO DO:

Show children either pictures of birds' nests or examples of old nests. Remind them that they should never touch or disturb a nest which is in use. Explain that the old ones are no longer used by the birds.

Talk about the types of birds that might have lived in the nests. Look closely at the nests, the materials they are made from and how they are made. If nests were seen on the Spring detecting walk, talk about them.

Show children a range of materials they might like to use to try making a nest. Encourage them to think about a particular bird. How big is it? Where might it build its nest? What materials would it use? Show children how twigs can be bent into a nest shape.

Ask the children to make a nest. If old nests or natural materials such as twigs and leaves are used remind children to wash their hands thoroughly after finishing the activity.

DISPLAY

Display the tree collages on a notice board. Place the nests on a table in front of the board. On another board begin the bulb timeline display described above. Place the vase of model daffodils and growing plants nearby.

Begin a display of the books read during the week and the group's version of *The Very Hungry Caterpillar.* As the topic progresses invite children to find other books for each week's theme.

Week 3

SPRING RAIN

PERSONAL AND SOCIAL DEVELOPMENT

• Use a picture of a rainy day or a poem to talk through feelings about rain. Talk about the kinds of clothes people wear in the rain and the need to wipe feet and remove outdoor clothing when coming inside. (PS8)

• Discuss ideas for keeping a teddy dry if it were to go outside in the rain. Encourage children to share ideas and to say why they think their solution will work - see activity opposite. (PS2, 4)

LANGUAGE AND LITERACY

• Prepare a large card cloud from which to hang card raindrops. Use a rain maker instrument to stimulate children to describe the sound of rain. Scribe the words on the raindrops. (L10)

• Enjoy sharing stories and poems about wet weather. (L2)

• Make a group big book about things children like to do in the rain. Encourage each child to draw a picture of what they like to do when it is raining. Under each picture scribe a sentence such as 'When it is wet I like to.....' or 'In the rain I like to.....'. Help children to write, trace or copy their name on the page. When the book is made share it with the group. (L1, 5, 12)

• Sing 'I hear thunder'. (L2)

MATHEMATICS

• Use the opportunity of water play to develop vocabulary related to capacity: full, empty, half full or half empty, more or less. (M1)

• Begin to measure capacity by counting how many small containers can be filled from one large one. Encourage children to predict and then count. Use the reverse procedure of counting how many times a small container can be filled and the water poured into a larger one. (M5, 6)

KNOWLEDGE AND UNDERSTANDING OF THE WORLD

• Use sieves, funnels and pots with holes to explore rain making. Which makes the largest drops? Which sound like rain on a very wet day? (K3, 5)

• Make rainy day pictures by painting on wet paper. Talk about what happens to the paint. (K3, 5)

• Talk about puddles. Where do they go? Draw around a puddle with chalk and observe it later in the day/week. (K5)

PHYSICAL DEVELOPMENT

• Talk about the way raindrops run down window panes. Use runny paint to do a blow painting. Ensure each child has a new straw. Encourage blowing not sucking! Discuss what the pictures remind children of. Ask each child to give their picture a title and scribe this for them. (PD3)

CREATIVE DEVELOPMENT

• Use tapping and clapping sounds to simulate a gentle trickle of rain, building up to a big storm then turning into a bright and sunny Spring day. (C1, 3)

• Make up a rain dance. (C3)

ACTIVITY:
Rainy clothes for teddy

Learning opportunity: Working as a group and independently, initiating ideas and solving problems.

Desirable Learning Outcome: Personal and Social Development. Children will share ideas for designing a waterproof suit for a teddy. Independently they will record their own ideas.

Resources: A teddy; a range of scraps of materials including ones which would be waterproof; examples of real rainwear; Teddy in the Rain poem; photocopied outlines of a teddy; pencils, crayons, felt pens.

Organisation: Whole group sitting comfortably on the floor.

Key vocabulary: Waterproof, umbrella, Wellington boots, raincoat, plastic, rubber.

WHAT TO DO:

Read the poem to the group.

Teddy in the Rain

**Outside it is raining
Teddy wants to be there,
But to keep his fur dry,
Special clothes he must wear.**

**He likes to splash in puddles,
Feel the rain upon his face,
And if his friend comes as well,
They will hold a sploshing race!**

**Teddy loves to be outside,
On a wet and rainy day,
So please help him decide
What to wear for rainy play!**

Talk about being outside in the rain. What kinds of clothes do children wear in the rain?

Invite one child to put on the rainwear clothes. Why are they good in the rain? From what sort of materials are they made? How do the materials look and feel? Show the teddy to the children. Ask what would happen to him if he went out in the rain. What would he need to wear to stay dry? Show children the scrap materials. Ask them to suggest which would be best for a raincoat.

Give each child one of the photocopied teddies. Invite them to design an outfit which would keep the teddy dry. Children could either do a collage with the scrap materials or they could colour with pens and crayons.

At the end of the session ask some children to show their pictures to the group and to explain why they have chosen the clothes and materials.

ACTIVITY: Tapping rain

Learning opportunity: Working collaboratively to make a rain tape.

Desirable Learning Outcome: Creative Development. Children will listen carefully to tapping sounds and use their hands to imitate the sounds of rain.

Organisation: Whole group sitting comfortably on the floor in a circle.

Key vocabulary: Pitter, patter, drip, drop, splish, splosh, splash.

WHAT TO DO:

Talk about the sound of rain. If you have a rain maker instrument, listen to the sound it makes as it is tipped.

Show children how they can tap two fingers of one hand gently against the palm of the other. What kind of rain does it sound like?

Explain that the group is going to try to make the sounds of rain by tapping with their fingers and by clapping. Explain that they must listen carefully and watch. Encourage them to tap gently, copying the sound of light rain, to tap progressively louder for heavier rain, to clap for a downpour and then become quieter until eventually the rain stops.

Repeat the performance and tape record the sounds. Play the tape back. Discuss whether it did sound like rain and whether the children might like to change any of the sounds.

DISPLAY

On a large piece of paper in the shape of an umbrella write out the 'Teddy in the Rain' poem. Display this with the children's teddy clothes designs. If there are too many designs to go on the display some could be placed in clear plastic wallets and put in a loose leaf file on a table by the board. Put the group's big book about the rain and the teddy on the table. Hang the cloud of rainy words near the board.

Week 4

WOOLLY WEEK

PERSONAL AND SOCIAL DEVELOPMENT

- If possible arrange a visit to a farm which has new lambs. Talk about caring for living creatures. (PS9)

LANGUAGE AND LITERACY

- Recite 'Little Bo Peep'. Talk about what it feels like to lose something which is precious. (L2)

- Draw attention to the rhymes in the poem. 'Peep' and 'sheep' both contain an 'ee' sound. Saying this sound makes us smile! Can the children think of any other words with this sound? Give clues: 'I saw a kitten the other day. It was fast asl........', or 'When it was rainy I stepped in a puddle which was very d...... '. (L7)

MATHEMATICS

- Play a simple number matching game with card sheep and a die labelled 1,1,2,2,3,3. Children pick up some sheep - they can choose to take one, two or three sheep. They then throw the die. If the number is the same as the number of sheep they took, they keep them. If not, they return their sheep to the pile. The game continues until no sheep are left. (M4, 5)

- Use the sheep counting rhyme - see activity opposite. (M3)

KNOWLEDGE AND UNDERSTANDING OF THE WORLD

- Talk about where wool comes from. Compare sheep's wool with wool bought from a shop. (K2, 3)

- Reinforce descriptive vocabulary relating to wool: soft, fluffy and warm. A piece of wool can be long or short. Which piece of wool is the softest? Can children find anything else in the room which is fluffy? (K2, 5, 7)

PHYSICAL DEVELOPMENT

- Use the context of sheep following each other to introduce a game of follow my leader. Encourage the leading sheep to use actions, clapping, skipping, hopping and steps of different sizes. Introduce simple obstacles, such as a hoop to climb through stepping stone mats, a skipping rope on the floor to walk along or a set of cones to weave between. (PD1, 2)

CREATIVE DEVELOPMENT

- Make paper plate wool weavings. (C1, 4)

- Make sheep collages by sticking white cotton wool balls on to green paper. Use black felt pen to add feet and a head to the sheep. Encourage children to use scraps of materials/draw to add other signs of Spring. (C1, 3)

ACTIVITY: Sheep counting rhyme

Learning opportunity: Using a counting rhyme for 1 to 5.

Desirable Learning Outcome: Mathematics. Children will be familiar with number rhymes and recognise and use numbers to ten.

Resources: None.

Organisation: Whole group sitting comfortably on the floor.

Key vocabulary: Numbers to five.

WHAT TO DO:

Talk to the children about shepherds. What do shepherds do? Talk about the importance of looking after sheep and of counting to check that none are lost. Pick five children and ask them to kneel on all fours pretending to be sheep. Walk around the sheep saying the following rhyme as you go:

A shepherd in his field one day,

Finds a sheep sitting in his way

He pats the sheep saying 'Come with me,
(Pat one sheep)

One sheep and I will go home for tea.'

The child who is patted wakes up and follows you Repeat the rhyme changing the last line to two, three, ... until all the sheep have gone home for tea.

As you demonstrate the rhyme encourage the children who are watching to join in with the words and to clap their hands on the word 'pats'. Once the children know what to do, a child can be the shepherd.

ACTIVITY: **Paper plate weaving**

Learning opportunity: Exploring colour and materials.

Desirable Learning Outcome: Creative Development. Children will explore colour and texture and use materials to express ideas.

Resources: Small paper plates or card circles, notched around the edge using pinking shears. Wools in a wide variety of Spring colours.

Organisation: Small group with adult supervision.

WHAT TO DO:

Talk to the children about the colours which are associated with Spring. Talk about the colours of blossom, Spring flowers and so on.

Explain to the children that they are going to make some wool weavings to show these Spring colours. Encourage each child to select the colours of wools which they would like to include in their weaving.

Help each child to start weaving by taping the end of

a long piece of their chosen wool to the back of their plate. Show how to wind the wool across the plate, catching it in the notches, so that the child ends up with something rather like the spokes of a bicycle wheel. Accuracy is not important. Now new colours and textures of wool can be woven between these spokes. Some children may enjoy weaving very carefully, but most will use the frame to hold pieces of wool in a fairly random manner. It does not matter. If the wools are thick and bright or fluffy all the results will be attractive.

As the children work, talk about the choices they are making. What does this colour remind you of? Does this wool feel quite the same as that one? Which wool is softer?

Encourage children to experiment with a variety of shades and textures. Some children may like to stick small twigs or coloured feathers into their pictures. Once mounted they can be used as the basis of Mothers' Day or Easter cards or just simply be appreciated as pictures of Spring.

DISPLAY

Make a display of children's clothes which are made from wool, balls of knitting wool, and books and pictures relating to sheep. Add captions which reinforce the processes involved in making woollen garments.

Week 5

MOTHERS' DAY

The topic of Mothers' Day should be dealt with sensitively so that no child feels excluded, whatever their personal circumstances. Mothers' Day should be viewed as an occasion when some people like to say thank-you to their mother but others may prefer to focus on someone else. An adult who is part of the group might talk about how they have not got a mother but they still send a card to ....

PERSONAL AND SOCIAL DEVELOPMENT

*   Use the 'Mother bakes' story opposite to discuss how 'little things matter'. (PS2, 4)

*   Read *Five Minutes' Peace* by Jill Murphy (Walker). Talk about the mother elephant. How could the children have been more helpful? Discuss the ways in which children can help their parents. (PS6)

LANGUAGE AND LITERACY

*   Help children to write a simple greeting and their name in a Mothers' Day card. (L10, 11, 12)

*   Talk to the children about all the different jobs which mums do.

    Encourage each child to paint a picture of their own mum busy doing one of these things. Perhaps there is something special which their Mum is interested in or is especially good at. Talk to the children about their pictures and scribe captions using the children's own words at the bottom of each. (L6)

MATHEMATICS

*   Use plastic animal families to practise sorting and grouping. Encourage the children to identify which animals they think are parents and young. How did they make their choices? (M1, 4)

*   As the children play with the animals encourage their use as a context for counting and problem solving. 'How many ducklings are following the

mother duck?' 'How many lambs does each mother sheep have? How many is that all together?' (M4)

KNOWLEDGE AND UNDERSTANDING OF THE WORLD

*   Talk about animal families, introducing and reinforcing the names of parents and young: a baby cat is a kitten, a baby horse is a foal and so on. Introduce some of the more specific names for male and female animals, such as cow and bull, mare and stallion. Reinforce the language by making a simple matching or happy families game. (K2)

*   Invite a parent or friend with a young baby to visit the group. How does the baby need to be looked after? What can the children do that the baby cannot? (K3)

PHYSICAL DEVELOPMENT

*   Hold a Mum's Choice Day. Invite mums, friends and carers to show the children some of the games which they enjoyed playing when they were young. Examples might be ring games such as 'The Farmer's in the Den', 'The Hokey Cokey', 'Oranges and Lemons', or simple playground games such as Grandmother's Footsteps. (PD1)

CREATIVE DEVELOPMENT

- Make a mug-shaped card for a Mothers' Day card - see activity below. (C1, 4)

ACTIVITY: Mother bakes

Learning opportunity: Working collaboratively. Initiating ideas.

Desirable Learning Outcome: Personal and Social Development. Children will mime to a story. They will discuss the meaning behind the story and suggest ideas of where 'little things make a difference'.

Organisation: Whole group sitting comfortably on the floor.

WHAT TO DO:

Explain that the group is going to mime to a story about a mother who decides to bake a tart. As you tell the story mime the baking, reading and so on. Encourage children to join in.

Mum finds a bowl, some flour, some water, some salt and some fat. She mixes them together to make pastry.

She rolls out the pastry, puts it in a pie dish, trims the edges, peels some apples and puts them in the dish. She covers it with more pastry, cuts it, pinches the edges and pops it in the oven.

While waiting for it to cook she reads a book. Suddenly she realises something smells nice. She puts on oven gloves and carefully takes the pie out. She cuts a slice, blows on it, and tastes. She shudders. It tastes horrible. She has forgotten to put the sugar on. It is sour!

The story is then repeated two more times. The second time she puts too much sugar on, the final time it is just right. She eats a slice, then another and so on until the pie has all gone, she feels full and falls asleep.

After the story talk to children about why only one pie tasted nice. Talk about the way just a small amount of sugar could make such a difference. Talk about little things children can do to make a difference such as picking up litter, saying 'please' and 'thank-you'.

ACTIVITY: Mothers' Day 'Have a tea break' cards

Learning opportunity: Exploring colour.

Desirable Learning Outcome: Creative Development. Children will make a card for a friend or relation exploring colours and communicating their feelings for the card receiver.

Resources: Crayons, pens and for each child a pre-cut mug-shaped card (see below) and a fruit tea-bag.

Organisation: Small group.

Key vocabulary: The names of colours, extending to include 'bright', 'dark', 'pastel' and 'deep'.

WHAT TO DO:

Show children the mug card and how a fruit tea-bag string can be inserted through a slit in the card. Explain that each child can make one to send to a mother, friend or relation.

Show children a variety of flavours of fruit tea-bags and encourage them to describe their scents. Which one would the person who will receive the card prefer?

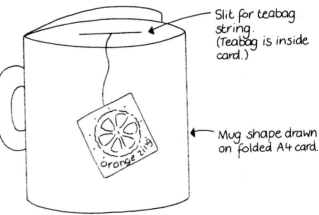

Slit for teabag string.
(Teabag is inside card.)

Mug shape drawn on folded A4 card.

orange zing

Provide each child with a mug card and ask them to decorate it. Encourage children to think about the person for whom they are making the card. What colours and patterns would they like? When it's completed each child can select a tea-bag for their card.

DISPLAY

Mount and display the children's paintings of their mums to make a small exhibition. How many mums recognise themselves?

Week 6

SPRING PARADE

PERSONAL AND SOCIAL DEVELOPMENT

- Explain to the children that they are going to invite friends, parents and carers to visit their group to see some of the work they have been doing during the last few weeks. Use the opportunity to recap some of the key experiences of the topic, reinforcing relevant vocabulary. Invite the children to identify personal highlights. (PS8, 10)

LANGUAGE AND LITERACY

- Involve the children in making invitations for the Spring parade. Encourage them to design and make their own cards but have ready-made photocopied 'inserts' giving relevant information, which can be glued inside each decorated card. (L6, 10)

- Work with the children to tell a collaborative, imaginative story. Begin with the discovery on the doorstep of a strange and wonderful egg. What do the children think it looked like? As you tell the story incorporate incidents which involve actions typical of individual children. Perhaps Amy took the egg to play with in the home corner, or Benji tried to play football with it. Stop at intervals to allow the children opportunity to contribute ideas and enjoy deciding together what will hatch out of the egg and the adventures to be had. Once started, you will find that the children will want to continue the story over several days. (L1, 2)

MATHEMATICS

- Prepare large, card egg shapes for children to decorate with bands of patterns. Provide printing blocks or pre-cut shapes to encourage the use of repeating patterns. Talk to the children about thepatterns they are making, the names of particular shapes, and the sequences being chosen. Which shape will come next? (M2)

KNOWLEDGE AND UNDERSTANDING OF THE WORLD

- Make and grow cress Spring bonnets - see activity opposite. (K3, 5, 8)

- Read *'Ahhh' said Stork* by Gerald Rose (MacMillan Picturemac) which tells the story of an egg found on the jungle floor. The jungle animals try unsuccessfully to break the egg to discover what is inside it. In the end a baby crocodile emerges, snapping his tiny teeth. Play a game in which you repeatedly find an egg. Give the children clues and allow them to guess what sort of animals will hatch from it. Encourage the children to suggest actions to represent the movements and sounds of the baby animal. (K2, K6)

PHYSICAL DEVELOPMENT

- Make musical egg shakers - see activity opposite. (PD3)

CREATIVE DEVELOPMENT

- Make Spring bonnets, hats or headbands.

- Use paper plates to form the basis of bonnets, with doilies or tissue paper flowers added and ribbons to tie.

- Make simple animal headband disguises by adding paper ears.

- Use grass made by fringing green paper to cover a headband and add spring animals, eggs or flowers. (C1)

cress.

card strip stuck around plastic tub

card circle stuck to the tub.

ACTIVITY:
Cress Spring bonnets

Learning opportunity: Selecting and cutting coloured paper. Observing cress seeds.

Desirable Learning Outcome: Knowledge and Understanding of the World. Children will make a Spring bonnet, sow cress seed and closely observe the seed as they grow.

Resources: Scissors, scraps of coloured papers, kitchen towel, cress seed, grown cress, double sided sticky tape and for each child a plastic tub inside a card bonnet as shown.

Organisation: Small group.

Key vocabulary: Sow, seed, shoot, grow.

WHAT TO DO:

Show children the card bonnets. Explain that they are each going to make a Spring bonnet in which to grow cress. Talk about how they might like to decorate their bonnet. Look at the papers. Which colours will they choose? Encourage children to decorate the bonnet sides and brim.

Show children some cress seed and a pot of grown cress. Ask them to describe what they see. Show them how to line the base of a pot with damp kitchen towel and how to sow cress seed thinly on the surface. Explain that each day children will need to look at their pot and to check the paper is still damp. Place the pots inside the bonnets and put them in a dark cupboard or cover them with a sheet of paper.

During the next few days children should be encouraged to observe the changes as the seeds swell and shoot. Once they have begun to shoot they should be placed in a light area.

NB It is best to do this activity at the start of a week so that the cress has time to shoot. The pots dry out quickly and should be taken home at the weekend.

ACTIVITY: Musical egg shakers

Learning opportunity: Children use materials to make musical instruments.

Desirable Learning Outcome: Physical Development. Children will handle objects and materials with increasing control.

Resources: A collection of the small plastic containers found in some children's chocolate eggs which contain small toys. Various materials to use as fillings (rice, dried peas, sand) in pots, with teaspoons for handling. Sequins; glitter; glitter glue pens or gummed shapes to decorate. A small selection of shaker instruments.

Organisation: Small groups.

Key vocabulary: Shake, rattle, beat, rhythm.

WHAT TO DO:

Show the children the shaker instruments with which they are already familiar. (You may even have some commercially produced shaking eggs.) Talk about how different instruments make slightly different sounds. Why do the children think this is so? Could it be that they have different things inside?

Explain to the children that they are going to make some shaker instruments of their own. Draw their attention to the plastic egg shapes, explaining that sadly they are empty! However, they are ideal for making small shakers which are easy for small hands to hold.

Talk to the children about the filling materials you have available and allow them to feel and handle them. Encourage each child to choose a filling for their personal shaker.

Show the children how to place a teaspoon of a chosen filling in one half of their shaker and then to fit the lid. These are often quite stiff and children will need adult help.

Encourage the children to then try out their shakers and to listen carefully to the sounds they can make. Do all the shakers make the same sound?

Suggest ways of decorating the outsides of the egg shakers.

Finally encourage children to shake the eggs rhythmically, perhaps adding stepping, foot tapping or singing or use them as an accompaniment to a nursery rhyme.

DISPLAY

Hang the completed bonnets around one of the seasonal displays. This provides a safe storage space and adds an attractive border to the existing work.

BRINGING IT ALL TOGETHER

INTRODUCING THE SPRING PARADE

Talk to the children about the idea of a Spring parade. This will be a simple event, possibly occupying the last half hour of a morning session, to which parents, carers and friends can be invited. The children will show some of the work they have been doing and there will be a few activities with a spring theme for visitors to share. Discuss how the children might make preparations for welcoming visitors and entertaining them.

INVOLVING THE CHILDREN IN PREPARATIONS

The introductory discussion will have helped children to understand that there are plenty of jobs to be done.

FOOD

Providing visitors with refreshments is not essential for a short event but it does present a purposeful context for children to develop simple culinary skills! Encourage the children to think about what sorts of food and drink might be appropriate. Ask them how they think the food should be presented. Decorate paper plates or paper tray covers in spring colours and patterns. (NB Care must be taken to avoid foods to which children may have allergies.)

Finger foods are easy for children to prepare:

- Use cress grown by the children to make cress, or egg and cress sandwiches.

- Preparing hard-boiled egg segments (perhaps served with a dip) gives an opportunity for children to observe changes caused by heat.

- Make Easter bonnet biscuits. Use icing as 'glue' to fix a large pink or white marshmallow sweet to the centre of a round biscuit. Drizzle icing over the 'brim' and decorate with tiny sweets or cake decorations.

- Make chocolate egg nests (see parent's page) to serve to guests.

- Allow children to make fruit cocktail drinks using a variety of juices with pieces of fruit to add panache! Encourage them to make decorated labels for the jugs, with pictures to represent the fruit juices used to make each drink.

INVITATIONS

Encourage the children to think about the information that they need to provide for the people they are inviting. You could collect children's ideas and make a photocopy of their suggestions to be pasted inside cards which children can decorate themselves. Alternatively highlight their ideas on a large sheet of paper which can be decorated by the children into a poster mural with Spring themes.

ACTIVITIES

- Egg shell collage:

  Make hard-boiled eggs using water containing food colourings. You can use the eggs to make sandwiches, but use the coloured shell pieces as a collage material to cover prepared shapes. Make sure the children wash their hands after handling egg shells.

- Decorating eggs:

  Provide hard-boiled eggs and a variety of papers, felt pens, shiny scraps and glue to decorate. Cut lengths of card cylinders from the inside of kitchen roll to make 'collars' in which to display the finished eggs. If you have a marbling tray, adults and children will enjoy producing beautiful designs on real or card eggs. If real eggs are used they will need to be placed in a 'holder' for dipping. This can easily be made from a pipe cleaner looped and twisted around the egg, with a free end left for holding.

- Spring parade:

  Many young children would become distressed at the suggestion of a formal musical hat parade. However, they can enjoy wearing their creations during this event, and if materials are provided they will have the opportunity to help visitors to make similar models for themselves!

SONGS:

A variety of Spring songs can be found in *Harlequin 44 Songs Round the Year* chosen by David Gadsby and Beatrice Harrop (A&C Black)

RESOURCES

RESOURCES TO COLLECT :

- A rain maker - a colourful version can be bought from an Early Learning Centre shop.

EVERYDAY RESOURCES:

- Boxes, large and small for modelling.
- Papers and cards of different weights, colours and textures - sugar, corrugated card, silver and shiny papers and so on.
- Dry powder paints for mixing and mixed paints for covering large areas such as card tree trunks.
- Different sized paint brushes from household brushes to thin brushes for delicate work and a variety of paint mixing containers.
- A variety of drawing and colouring pencils, crayons, pastels, charcoals, etc.
- Additional decorative and finishing materials such as sequins, foils, glitter, tinsel, shiny wool and threads, beads, pieces of textiles, parcel ribbon.
- Table covers.

STORIES

Beaky by Jez Alborough (Walker).

The Tiny Seed by Eric Carle (Hamish Hamilton/Puffin Books).

The Very Hungry Caterpillar by Eric Carle (Picture Puffins).

The Trouble with Dad by Babette Cole (Mammoth).

The Trouble with Mum by Babette Cole (Picture Lions).

Hepzibah's Woolly Fleece by Jill Dow (Frances Lincoln Ltd).

A Hard Day's Work by Mick Gowar (Delacorte Press).

Alfie's Feet by Shirley Hughes (The Bodley Head).

Billy's Beetle by Mick Inkpen (Hodder and Stoughton).

Emma's Lamb by Kim Lewis (Walker).

Floss by Kim Lewis (Walker).

The Shepherd Boy by Kim Lewis (Walker).

Five Minutes' Peace by Jill Murphy (Walker).

Who am I? by Judith Nicholls (Ladybird).

'Ahhh' said Stork by Gerald Rose (Macmillan Picturemac).

POETRY BOOKS

This Little Puffin by Elizabeth Matterson (Puffin).

Out and About by Shirley Hughes (Walker).

Over and Over Again. Poems and songs for the very young by Barbara Ireson and Christopher Rowe (Beaver Books).

POSTERS

The Seasons - pack of four posters from *Practical Pre-School*.

NON-FICTION

Tadpole and Frog by Christine Back and Barrie Watts (A & C Black).   Good for pictures.

The Egg created by Pascale de Bourgoing and Gallimard Jeunesse (Moonlight Publishing/First Discovery).

Pond Life by Barbara Taylor (Dorling Kindersley). Good for pictures.

INFORMATION FOR ADULTS

Spring Tinderbox compiled by Chris Deshpande and Julia Eccleshare (A & C Black).

The Seasons by Rosie Harlow and Gareth Morgan (Kingfisher).

Spring Festivals by Mike Rosen (Wayland).

COLLECTING EVIDENCE OF CHILDREN'S LEARNING

Monitoring children's development is an important task. Keeping a record of children's achievements will help you to see progress and will draw attention to those who are having difficulties for some reason. If a child needs additional professional help, such as speech therapy, your records will provide valuable evidence.

Records should be the result of collaboration between group leaders, parents and carers. Parents should be made aware of your record keeping policies when their child joins your group. Show them the type of records you are keeping and make sure they understand that they have an opportunity to contribute. As a general rule, your records should form an open document. Any parent should have access to records relating to his or her child. Take regular opportunities to talk to parents about children's progress. If you have formal discussions regarding children about whom you have particular concerns, a dated record of the main points should be kept.

KEEPING IT MANAGEABLE

Records should be helpful in informing group leaders, adult helpers and parents and always be for the benefit of the child. However, keeping records of every aspect of each child's development can become a difficult task. The sample shown will help to keep records manageable and useful. The golden rule is to keep them simple.

Observations will basically fall into three categories:

- **Spontaneous records:** Sometimes you will want to make a note of observations as they happen, for example, if a child is heard counting cars accurately during a play activity, or is seen to play collaboratively for the first time.

- **Planned observations:** Sometimes you will plan to make observations of children's developing skills in their everyday activities. Using the learning opportunity identified for an activity will help you to make appropriate judgements about children's capabilities and to record them systematically.

To collect information:

- talk to children about their activities and listen to their responses;

- listen to children talking to each other;

- observe children's work such as early writing, drawings, paintings and 3-D models. (Keeping photocopies or photographs is sometimes useful.)

Sometimes you may wish to set up 'one off' activities for the purposes of monitoring development. Some groups, for example, ask children to make a drawing of themselves at the beginning of each term to record their progressing skills in both co-ordination and observation. Do not attempt to make records following every activity!

- **Reflective observations:** It is useful to spend regular time reflecting on the progress of a few children (aim for about four children each week). Aim to make some brief comments about each child every half term.

INFORMING YOUR PLANNING

Collecting evidence about children's progress is time consuming and it is important that it is useful. When you are planning, use the information you have collected to help you to decide what learning opportunities you need to provide next for children. For example, a child who has poor pencil or brush control will benefit from more play with dough or construction toys to build the strength of hand muscles.

Example of recording chart

Name: Alice Field		D.O.B. 26.2.95		Date of entry: 13.9.98	
Term	**Personal and Social**	**Language and Literacy**	**Mathematics**	**Knowledge and understanding**	**Physical**	**Creative**
ONE	Keen to see frog spawn change. Anxious to return tadpoles to pond. 20.4.99 EHL	Enjoying listening to poems. Those by Shirley Hughes are particular favourites. 20.3.99	Was able to carry out addition by counting on objects. 26.2.99 LSS	Interested in story of wool. Brought in knitted doll. 16.3.99 AC	Show good control with blow painting. Finding balancing difficult. 16.2.99 AC	Enjoyed the challenge of weaving - showed great perseverance. 2.3.99 LSS
TWO						
THREE						

SKILLS OVERVIEW OF SIX WEEK PLAN

Week	Topic focus	Personal and Social	Language and Literacy	Mathematics	Knowledge and Understanding of the World	Physical	Creative
1	Detecting Spring	Appreciating the environment Being sensitive to others	Talking Listening Role play	Counting Number recognition	Observing Recording	Moving imaginatively Increasing control	Handling materials
2	Frogs	Treating living things with care and concern	Listening Writing Talking	Counting	Comparing Observing	Jumping	Collaborative building
3	Spring rain	Problem solving Sharing ideas	Discussing Writing	Developing language Measuring	Comparing Observing	Handling materials with control	Composing music Dancing
4	Woolly week	Treating living things with care and concern	Rhyming	Counting	Observing Comparing	Moving with imagination and awareness of space	Working with a variety of materials
5	Mothers' Day	Helping others Discussing feelings	Discussing Describing Early writing	Sorting Grouping Problem solving	Language development Comparing	Playing games collaboratively	Cutting and folding
6	Spring parade	Developing new ideas	Knowing that words and pictures carry meaning Early writing	Recognising shapes Patterns	Comparing Observing Questioning	Using materials with control Moving with imagination	Folding Cutting Joining

HOME LINKS

The theme of Spring lends itself to useful links with children's homes and families. Through working together children and adults gain respect for each other and build comfortable and confident relationships.

RESOURCE REQUESTS

- Make a collection of the plastic egg-shaped containers from the insides of chocolate eggs. These are for making shakers.

- Additional plastic farm animals or pictures of farm animals will be useful.

ESTABLISHING PARTNERSHIPS

- Keep parents informed about the topic of Spring, and the themes for each week. By understanding the work of the group, parents will enjoy the involvement of contributing ideas, time and resources.

- Photocopy the parent's page for each child to take home. This will give parents additional information which will enable them to support the topic through shared activities, encouraging children to be aware of seasonal changes in their environment.

- Invite friends, carers and families to attend the Spring parade.

GROUP VISITORS

- In Mother's Day week, invite mums and carers to suggest favourite games for the children to play.

- During the same week, it is suggested that a mother and baby be invited to the group to talk about meeting a baby's needs.

- Invite keen gardeners to talk to the children about choosing and growing seeds.

PREPARING THE SPRING PARADE

- Help may be needed in supporting children as they make their spring bonnets. At the event it will be helpful to have additional adult helpers to assist children as they take charge of their games and stalls.